Nestor in Portugal, Discoveries

Early Reader
Children's Picture Books

Written By: Margarida Teixeira
Illustrated By: Kissel Cablayda

JD-Biz Publishing

Download Free Books!

http://MendonCottageBooks.com

All Rights Reserved.

No part of this publication may be reproduced in any form or by any means, including scanning, photocopying, or otherwise without prior written permission from JD-Biz Corp and Mendon Cottage LLC Copyright © 2017

All Images Licensed by Mendon Cottage LLC and Kissel Cablayda

Read More Mendon Cottage Books

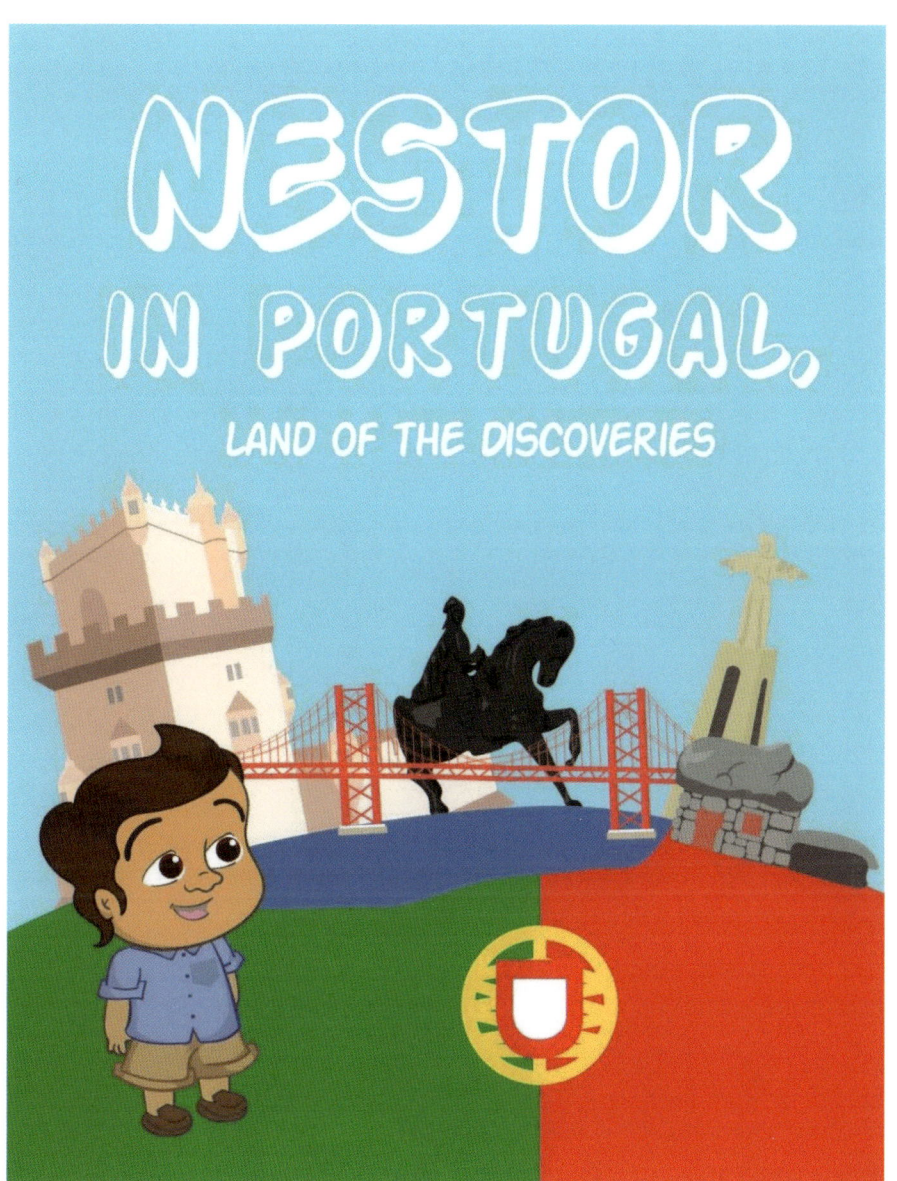

Nestor loves to discover other cultures and people. His parents are diplomats. That means they change houses and countries a lot. Nestor always goes with them and gets to see lots of interesting stuff!

This time, Nestor's dad told him they are going to Portugal. "Where is Portugal?" asks Nestor. "It is a country in the Iberian Peninsula, between Spain and the Atlantic Ocean."

"Oh, so they speak Spanish!" says Nestor. "No, they speak Portuguese. Portuguese is the 6th most spoken language in the world…but a lot of people still think it is the same as Spanish!" sighed dad.

They arrive in Lisbon on a sunny summer day. Nestor is dazzled. At first, when he sees the red bridge, he thinks he is in San Francisco.

"No, but it was the same architect who created both bridges!" smiles mom, "That's why they look so similar!"

Their apartment is in the old part of Lisbon. You can see the river through the balcony and the streets are very narrow and colorful. You can also see a castle on top of a hill.

"Please, mom and dad, can we go see the castle?" asks Nestor. He loves all things medieval and he likes to compare the different castles he has seen.

Nestor and his parents go walking towards the castle. Lisbon is said to have seven hills, so they have to go up and down a lot. The sidewalk is also very special, it is called calçada and there are drawings on it.

When they finally get to the castle, Nestor is very happy. He goes on to discover the castle walls and he loves to go on top of the towers, where he has the best view of the city.

"This is amazing!" says Nestor "It feels like I can touch the ocean!" "It's not an ocean," corrects dad, "it's a river. But the river in Lisbon flows into the Atlantic Ocean, that is why it looks like the sea."

After walking through the castle, Nestor and his parents decide to go downtown and take the tram to Belém.

Many of the ships of the Discovery age started their voyage in this old neighborhood in Lisbon, so Nestor feels very dreamy when he sees the old Belém Tower and the Monastery of Jeronimos.

After that, they take another train and they go to Sintra, a lovely town on the outskirts of Lisbon. It is very colorful and there are plenty of palaces and haunted places. It seems like a fairytale to Nestor!

After visiting Lisbon for a few days, Nestor must begin his studies. He knows Spanish so Portuguese lessons aren't very hard for him, although it still sounds weird. His classmates make fun of his Spanish accent.

Nestor goes to a bilingual school across the river. That means he has to cross the bridge every day. He loves looking at the landscape when he is in the car with his parents – everything seems so monumental and beautiful!

The place where Nestor goes to school is called Arrábida and it is on a mountain range by the ocean. One day, he goes on a school trip to discover the mountains and they finish the day by the sea.

The beaches in Arrábida are very different from what he is used to. The sand is very white and there are a lot of cliffs. In those cliffs there are deep forests where people go hiking.

Nestor loves the sea, but he is shocked to discover how cold the water is! He thinks the Atlantic ocean is a lot colder than other bodies of water he has swam in, but he gets used to it quickly.

During the winter, his parents decide to take him on a trip to the northern portion of Portugal. There, he discovers a village lost in the countryside where they still have pagan rituals.

Men and boys dress like demons; they perform secret mischievous acts during the Christmas season. Nestor immediately wants to try to do the same and so he dresses up as a Careto.

Since the North of Portugal has old Celtic influences, sometimes Nestor thinks he is in Ireland. Everything is very green and the coast has a rough sea.

Several months later, in the summer, his parents decide to take him on a tour of the Southern part of Portugal. It is quite different. Alentejo almost looks like a desert, while Algarve is full of beach resorts.

His parents also take him to an Arab village called Mértola. The Arabs have inhabited Portugal for centuries. Nestor likes hearing the stories of those days of adventure and fighting.

When it comes time to leave, Nestor is sad. He will miss the sunny days in Lisbon and the diversity of Portugal, a small country where the landscape can change drastically over a few miles.

Thankfully, his last days in Lisbon are during the popular holidays of Santos Populares. And so he leaves the country, his heart filled with joy, when people are singing and dancing in the streets and eating sardines like there is no tomorrow.

Author Bio

Margarida Teixeira

Margarida studied Philosophy and Human Rights and currently lives in France.

Illustrator Bio

Kissel Cablayda is a full time graphic artist and painter based in Davao City, Philippines. When she was 9, she won from a school editorial cartooning contest and from that day on she knew her world will revolve in arts and design. Eleven years later, she graduated with a degree in Bachelor of Arts in Communication Arts Major in Media Arts from the University of the Philippines Mindanao.

Her first and second job was terrible. So she decided to have a homebased job and find her passion. Now she happily works as an online book illustrator at Mendon Cottage Books.

She believes that creativity is a journey, not a destination, and that design is an essential part of every human communication and experience. She also believes that unicorns are real.

When she is not designing, she spends her time travelling, watching TV series, reading a bunch of books and cleaning her room. She likes novels written by Chaim Potok, Sidney Sheldon and Harper Lee. She loves Filipino meat cuisine and hates vegetables.

She aspires to excel in her career and make other people's lives be less hard through art and design.

To know more about her, email her at kisselcablayda2013@gmail.com

Download Free Books!
http://MendonCottageBooks.com

Nestor in Portugal, land of the Discoveries

Nestor in Portugal, land of the Discoveries Page 32

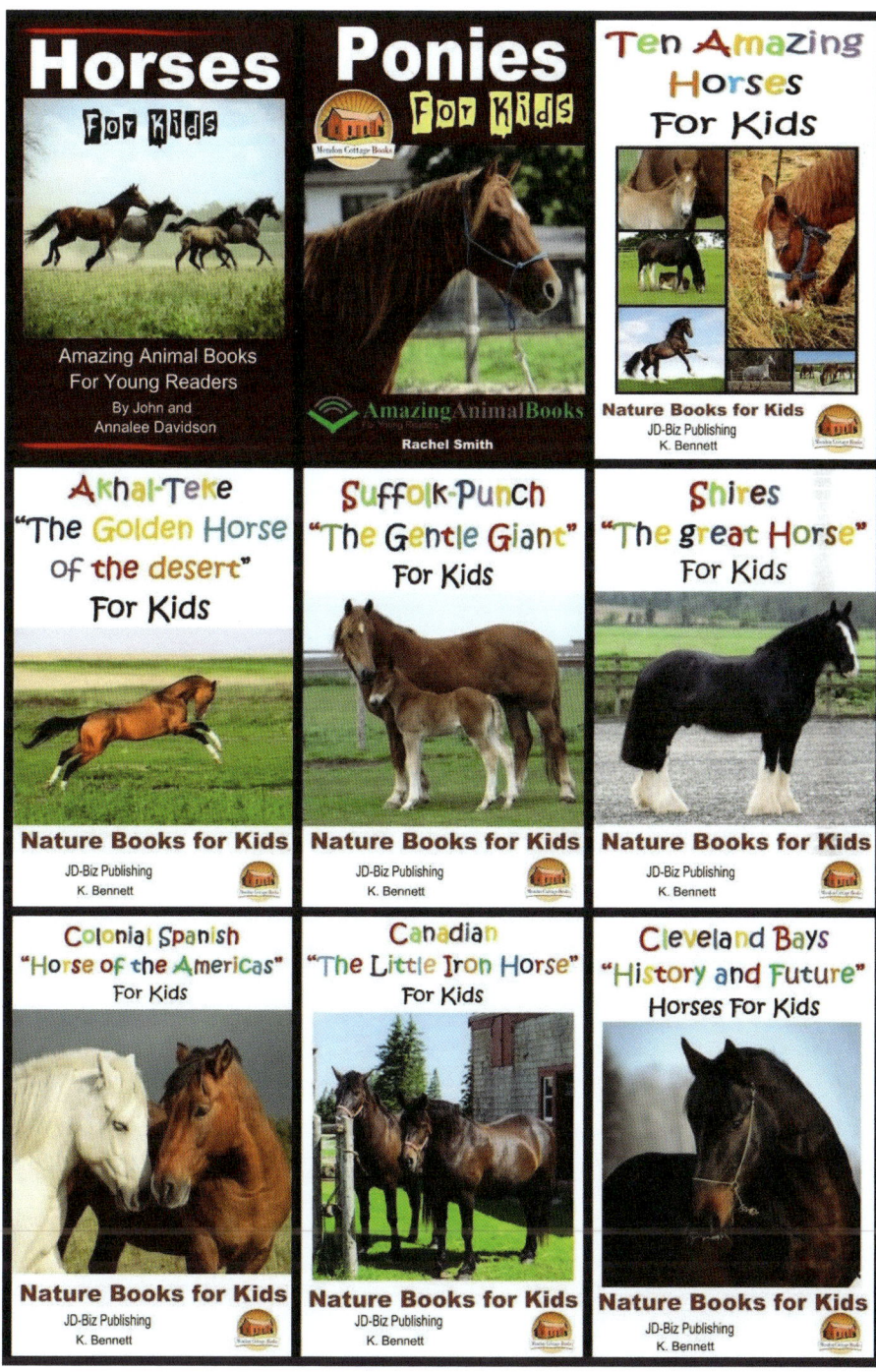

Nestor in Portugal, land of the Discoveries		Page 33

Nestor in Portugal, land of the Discoveries

Our books are available at

1. Amazon.com
2. Barnes and Noble
3. Itunes
4. Kobo
5. Smashwords
6. Google Play Books

Download Free Books!
http://MendonCottageBooks.com

Publisher

JD-Biz Corp

P O Box 374

Mendon, Utah 84325

http://www.jd-biz.com/

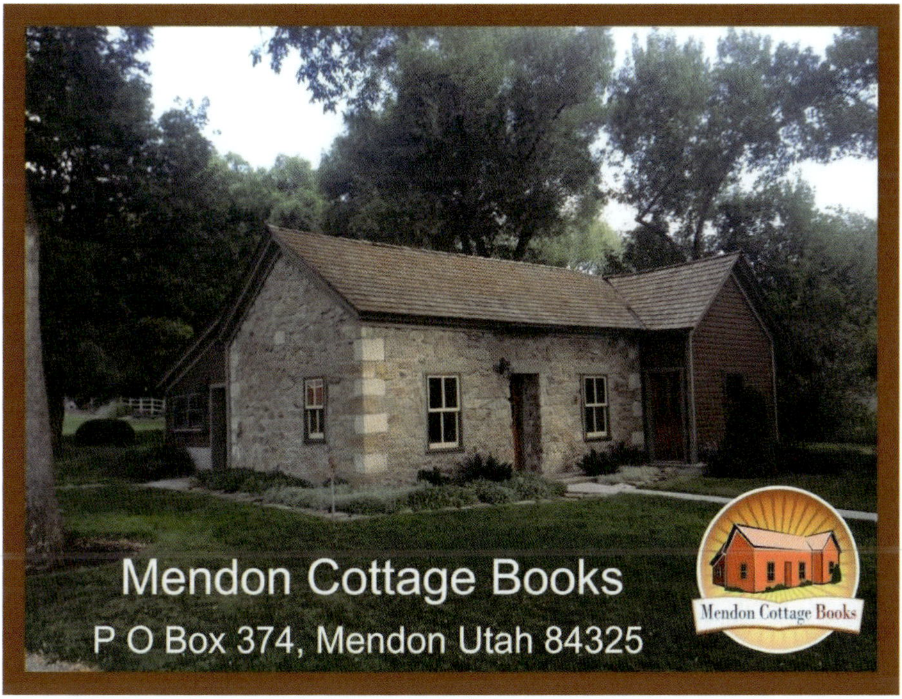

Printed in Poland
by Amazon Fulfillment
Poland Sp. z o.o., Wrocław